BLUE
PULLMAN

Supplement

Contents

© Kevin Robertson and Noodle Books 2009

ISBN 978-1-906419-24-0

First published in 2009 by Kevin Robertson
under the **NOODLE BOOKS** imprint
PO Box 279
Corhampton
SOUTHAMPTON
SO32 3ZX

www.kevinrobertsonbooks.co.uk

Printed in England by the Information Press

Front cover - *The 'Bristol Pullman' west of Chippenham, circa 1965/66.*

John Palk

Preceding pages - *The afternoon up Bristol Pullman, (3.15pm ex Bristol),22nd September 1961, passing Morton Sidings east of Didcot. The period from 1960 to 1964 was the undoubted heyday of these trains, their novelty factor allied to the attraction they presented in striking livery, with on board personal service represented an time that would never be repeated. In the background, 57XX 0-6-0PT No 8730 waits to leave the site on a Reading bound freight.*

Michael Mensing

Opposite - *The cavernous interior of Bristol Temple Meads, with a London bound train depicted prior to departure. The shades over the side running lights will be noted, as will the connected shore supply.*

Rear cover - *Towards the end of operational service, an 8-car Bristol working, but with a former Midland Pullman power car leading, approaches Twerton Tunnel.*

Dave Walden

INTRODUCTION

     I can truthfully say I was staggered by the response to my original *BLUE PULLMAN book*. To be fair, at the time the topic was somewhat fashionable amongst enthusiasts and modellers, the latter ever hopeful one of the major manufacturers might well introduce a ready to run 4mm version. In the larger ''O' scale, the enthusiast is better catered for, albeit in kit form. Regretfully, in the smaller scale, nothing has yet appeared, although I can appreciate the difficulties such a product would create, considering the variations between the LMR and WR power cars, let alone the trailer cars. Fortunately, in book form, matters are easier to resolve.

     As with any book, when the time comes to 'call a halt' there will inevitably be questions remaining. Often these were unknown when research commenced, whilst new material will also appear later as a result of publication. This was certainly the case following the release of the original book and provides the opportunity for a further, mainly pictorial, album of what, I hope, are previously unpublished scenes, as well as providing the opportunity to answer some previously raised questions. Additionally, a number of new colour pictures have been located and it is appropriate also to include these.

     My thanks are due to all who have contacted me offering comment, criticism and, of course, further information. Their names, together with an addenda to the original book, are mentioned on the final page.

     As before, I hope what follows will be of interest. A tribute to what can only be described as *the* truly iconic train-sets of the 1960s.

Kevin Robertson

PULLMAN DE LUXE HIGH SPEED TRAINS

Think of Blue Pullman today and you are considering a design more than 50 years, half a century, old. A design which when compared now with twenty-first century fashion, appears out moded and out dated, yet which, just those same 50 years ago, was pushing the boundaries of design technology in many areas. Hence, according officially to Metropolitan-Cammell, the trains were known as, 'The British Transport Commission Pullman De Luxe High Speed Trains'. Indeed, in the 1970s and after the actual units had been consigned to scrap, some of older Metropolitan-Cammell employees still referred to the units as 'The High Speed', notwithstanding that already, the genuine high-speed train sets had been rolled off the production line and were in service on British Railways.

But as the reader may have gathered, from the opening paragraph above, it may seem as if the history, operation and demise of the 36 vehicles making up the five Blue Pullman sets had been condensed into one short set of words. That is certainly not the intention. So we will return to the 1960s and to what has been described by one correspondent as "...A splendid train that should be a source of pride to those who were involved in its creation."

A source of pride then to the manufacturers and workers. Yes indeed for, as has been stated previously, nothing like it had been seen before and it certainly displayed a potential for forward thinking 50 years ago. But how did the professional commentators of the day respond to the actual train in service? We can turn to people such as G Freeman Allen, who, in the August 1960 issue of *Trains Illustrated,* noted, "On the basis of a few miles running over a route whose track may be below the best British standards, it might be unfair to pronounce the unequivocal opinion on the new Pullmans' ride. I will content myself with a suggestion that this is not in the same European class as the Pullmans' furnishings....."

Freeman Allen does not appear to have referred to the service involved, although this must have been the Midland route, as the service from Paddington did not start until September 1960. (There was of course always the possibility that Freeman Allan had been privileged to travel on one of the WR press trips, but this appears unlikely.)

Next to enter the debate was Cecil J Allen, writing in the same periodical, but this time the October 1960 issue. "As to the riding of the stock, however, although this is certainly good, it could not be said that perfection has yet been attained."

In the same October 1960 issue, an un-named contributor appeared to take issue with the earlier views expressed by G Freeman Allen. "A trip in the Midland Pullman in regular service has modified slightly some of the opinions expressed in our August issue description of the new diesel-electric Pullman units. In a few places between St Pancras and Leicester, notably in the first few miles out of the London terminus, the riding was boisterous, but the track must certainly take some of the blame here....."

But although BR may well have hoped for the train-sets to effect a 'settling down' in service, possibly even with their luxury décor, the word 'opulent' is perhaps inappropriate when referring to 1960's and service compensating for the shortcomings, this did not appear to happen. Indeed Brain Haresnape, again in *Trains Illustrated,* this time the April 1961 issue, commented, "...one worrying feature is that when in motion, empty seats tend to vibrate incessantly."

Finally in this collection of whinges comes this comment from Margaret Wilson, in her article 'Three years of the Blue Pullmans' - *Modern Railways,* July 1963. "The cooking staff appreciate the train's speed and smoothness in acceleration and deceleration; they greatly dislike its occasional exuberance in riding, however, which they allege is transmitted from coach to coach through incorrectly adjusted couplers. If the bogie modifications being carried out at Derby remove this cause for complaint, they will probably enjoy the best working conditions among train catering crews

Left - A wonderful image and which in many ways, portrays the changing image of the 1960s railway. Gone is steam and instead modern diesel units are providing the service. The concrete flower tubs provide a further degree of modernity, yet the retention of the semaphore signals and timber sleepered bull-head track are not out of place. This was the modern railway, to many, aesthetically at least, at its most visually attractive. It was also the peak period for the Blue Pullman sets on the Western Region. The down train is seen here entering Leamington Spa General, on what was always the more important of the WR Blue Pullman services, that covering the Birmingham route.

Lawrence Hassall / KR Collection

on British Railways."

A more official record of the problems associated with the riding of the vehicles comes from Malcolm Botham, at the time employed by Metropolitan-Cammell as a Junior Engineer. Reporting to Senior Engineer, John Thring, who in turn reported to the Chief Engineer, J L R Barmes. Malcolm's role was to trouble-shoot the problems associated with the rough riding, particularly of the power cars, which was apparent immediately after they entered service.

Malcolm has kindly reported his recollections of the runs made, which make for fascinating reading.

"The ride problems were wholly with the power bogies. The Schlieren trailers were good riding, although a little short of the quality achieved by today's designs.

"Weight alone was not a fundamental problem. Rather more it was weight distribution. But there were some serious design defects.

1. Passenger compartment at the rear end of the power car.
2. Heavy weight at the leading end of the power car caused the power bogies to be located at the rear end of the power car and the other at the end of the trailer car adjacent to the power car.
3. Disposition of drives between traction motors and axles.

"Having the passenger compartment at the rear end of the power car caused the weight of the heavy diesel engine and generator set to be disposed considerably towards the driving cab from the geometric centre between bogies of the car body. Pitch and yaw motions of the car body are natural vibration modes, pitch being the rotational movement about the horizontal axis laterally through the centre of gravity of the body and yaw being the rotational movement about the vertical axis, also through the centre of gravity. Since this centre of gravity was disposed towards the driving cab end of the vehicle, the movements at the passenger compartment were much greater than those at

the cab end. Thus whilst passengers were having their coffee and soup spilt in their laps, the driver was enjoying a comfortable ride.

"The reason for locating the second power bogie on the trailer car was that to put it at the leading end of the power car would have caused the axle load at this end to have exceeded the allowable limit, at this time, I believe, 17.5 tons.

"The drives between traction motors and axles were of a design by Brown Boveri of Switzerland used on Swiss locomotives. The traction motors were attached to the bogie frames and were thus part of the sprung mass via the primary suspension. They drove the axles through quill drives. These were arrangements of coil springs disposed radially around the drives and could thus accommodate the vertical movements between bogie frames and axles. I believe this to be an innovation to BR, where traction motors were hung partly on the axles and partly on the bogie frames, the Chief Civil Engineer was no doubt delighted at the prospect of having less damaging shocks transmitted to his tracks.

"It was not the practice in those days to carry out extensive ride tests before vehicles entered passenger service. Indeed, Metro-Cammell had no facilities for such testing and BR had only service tracks on which to do so. Thus the Blue Pullmans entered service straight from the drawing board, as it were, although there may have been some limited test running, eg between the works and Derby." (We know press photographs at least were taken on the Wirksworth branch, although it would be unlikely any reasonable speed could have been achieved on this line.)

"Thus it was, after complaints from irate passengers, that BR decided to run tests between Leicester and Bedford, part of the route operated by the 6-car Manchester Pullman. The 'spare' 6-car train was stabled at Derby and thus had to run to Leicester for the tests proper to begin. I was deputed always to start with it from Derby.

"I recall the first test run I went on. The senior Metropolitan Cammell man present was

Left - St Pancras, with one of the six car Midland Pullman sets apparently just departing. The identity of the power car concerned is not known, although it is very unusual as there is only one windscreen wiper fitted. This may appear to be a trivial issue, but a study of all available photographs appears to reveal that only one of the Midland sets was thus supplied and as the trains did not have set numbers shown, it makes identification very difficult. It is probably reasonable to conclude that a second wiper was added later and this was indeed the only power car to appear in this form. The all important tea-can will be noted.

Lawrence Hassall / KR Collection

W60099 at the head of the 8-coach 'Bristol Pullman' standing at Bath Spa in the early 1960s. The set is clean although clearly slightly travel stained. At the rear of the power car, the 18 seat second-class compartment would appear to be well filled. Experience in alterations to the damping of the Midland Region sets would, of course, have also been applied to the Western Region units, although as far as some passengers were concerned, the importance of being able to secure a quick exit through the ticket barrier at Paddington by occupying seats in the first coach seemed to outweigh any disadvantage so far as the ride was concerned. To be fair, the ride quality associated with Western Region track was also far superior to that on the Midland lines. The 'Blue Pullman' sets have often been referred to as the forerunners to the later HSTs, although it perhaps dangerous to attempt to draw to many comparisons in this area. One lesson that was learnt and applied was, of course, in relation to the rear of the power car on the HST sets which was not given over to passenger accommodation.

Tony Woodforth collection

the Chief Railcar Draughtsman, Charlie Large. The journey from Derby to Leicester was uneventful but, shortly after the test proper was started, the ride got rougher and loud staccato banging was heard coming from beneath the floor above the power bogie of the power car. These bangs lasted no more than a few seconds, but recurred a number of times during the run. Charlie and I were at a loss to explain them.

"Also on the test was the representative of Armstrong Dampers, who had supplied the dampers for the primary suspension. He was enormously helpful throughout the tests and I am ashamed to say I cannot remember his name. I will call him Mr A. The Armstrong dampers were of the arm type, as opposed to telescopic. They were not adjustable without

disassembling them and changing the interior valving, but Mr A said he could lay his hands on a set of experimental dampers which were easily adjustable through a knob on the outside of their casings. We eagerly accepted this offer and asked BR to arrange further test runs. This was not an easy and quick thing to do, since they had to produce a leaflet (Special Traffic Notice), giving route and timetable information and likewise circulate it to all operating staff involved, eg signalmen. Thus the tests were carried out over a prolonged period, since no-one could predict how many test runs were to be needed. My memory suggests that this was months rather than weeks.

"It should be appreciated that dampers were often misnamed 'shock absorbers'. They were nothing of the sort. Rather they were

Late morning at St Pancras. The service from Manchester has already disgorged its passengers and will now be prepared for the fill-in Nottingham working.

'shock transmitters'. Thus the downside to increasing the damping forces was to increase the intensity of shocks coming from transient events in the track, such as rail joints, switches and crossings. Nevertheless, such increased damping could reduce the amplitude of vibrations across the springs particularly if a resonant mode was being picked up. Since we are considering the primary suspension, these shocks would be transmitted into the bogie frames, but the car bodies had the added protection of the secondary springs and would not therefore experience so much of these shocks.

"When the next series of tests, with the adjustable dampers, began they were attended by the British Railways Board (BRB) representative, the late, to my mind great, J L Koffman. Koffman reported directly to the BRB CM&EE, F (Freddie) Harrison and his assistant E S Cox. Koffman was a prolific writer of articles on railway dynamics published in *The Railway Gazette* and other journals, thus I knew him by repute. These articles were usually highly mathematical and were of great assistance and inspiration to me. In those days, railway vehicle design was the preserve of the Chief Engineer, Chief Draughtsman and senior section leaders

in the drawing office. Many of them pooh-poohed the Koffman articles, since their designs relied on experience and intuition and, anyway, they could neither understand nor apply the mathematical formulae.

"Lacking their experience, but strong on maths, the Koffman articles were what I needed to be able to make a contribution. When I met Koffman for the first time, it was with feelings of awe and trepidation, but I need not have worried. When I told him I had been trying to apply his formulae to the present problem, he was most supportive and friendly and I was greatly encouraged by this.

"I would always join the train at Derby together with Mr A, who had by now fitted the adjustable dampers, and we would then agree the settings for the next test run. We would use one setting for the run from Leicester to Bedford and then change it for the run back to Leicester. To start with all dampers were set to identical strength and these were increased in small steps at a time for subsequent test runs. Koffman would join the train at Leicester, as would my own boss, John Thring.

"The next few runs produced little improvement, except that the intensity and frequency of occurrence of the staccato

Above - *An almost spotless set at Long Eaton Junction south of Nottingham, working the 3.30 pm Nottingham Midland to St Pancras, Wednesday 13th April 1966, just two days before services ceased on the LMR.* Bill Chapman

Arrival again at St Pancras, undated, but possibly not long after the service commenced. Forty odd years later and the station would be transformed. Multiple units sets still arrive, although the prestige services of the 21st century are destined for slightly further afield than Manchester as well as heading in a different direction. (Eurostar of course).

hangings were diminishing with the increasing damping. But there was little improvement in the general ride. Around the same time, I was attempting to do calculations, to see if I could determine the source of the problem. I decided it was probably due to excessive bogie frame pitching, but the realisation came that the springs of the Brown-Boveri quill drives were having an influence. Effectively, they were in parallel with the primary suspension springs and because the quill drives were diagonally disposed, they were causing the primary suspension at two diagonal corners of the bogie to be stiffer than those at the other two. The effect of this on bogie frame pitching was to force it to occur on an axis effectively rotated at an angle to the pure lateral axis. The increased pitching motion at two corners was causing these to hit the limiting stops and thus produce the banging. My plan was to increase the damping force at two corners and reduce it at the other two.

"My solution was not a theoretically purist one, which would have required substantial modifications. One cannot alter the stiffness of a spring / mass system by changing the damping force across it. Thus one could not change the frequency of its vibrations, at least not until the damping approached its critical value, which would be quite unacceptable since that would be akin to having no spring at all and the shocks transmitted would be most violent.

"More test runs followed on the basis of trying out this differential damping and, if it proved efficacious in principle, to optimise the damper settings.

"It worked. Kofftman agreed to it and perhaps I had acquired some of the experience and intuition previously lacking. Having found the optimum damper settings, the test dampers and all those on the remaining power bogies were replaced by permanently set ones in the differential disposition. Although the ride over the power bogies was never as good as on the

Left - *Westbound from Chippenham in what were certainly the halcyon days for the service. The goods stock on the right might even be taken for a reminder as to the instruction that tail traffic was not to be taken on the Pullman units. In reality did staff really need reminding?*

Peter Elliott / K R Collection

13

The 1960 Pullman Car Company Christmas card and of course featuring the new trains. Bearing in mind the time of year it was perhaps a pity a snow scene was not used.

One of the five Diesel Electric Pullmans built by Metropolitan-Cammell Carriage and Wagon Company Limited, England

GREETINGS

and Good Wishes for a Happy Christmas and Good Cheer in the New Year

1960-1961

THE PULLMAN CAR COMPANY LIMITED

' Good Cheer on the journey maketh the way seem shorter '

Included for the purpose of displaying the Pullman livery of course! The view is a very good rendition of the original 'Nanking' blue and white colour scheme used for both the Midland and Western sets. One slight puzzle is the reference in the background to seats 1-9. Seen is a WR set and Coach 'D' was thus a Parlour First seating 36 persons and as with all the trains, having doors only at the ends. (The provision of coach letters may have been an after-thought as views of the 6-car sets on trial do not appear to display these. They were present, however, on the WR sets from the start of the public service.) To the left is Gerald Fiennes, one time General Manager of the Western Region and variously described as "The best Chairman British Railways never had".

trailer bogies, at least the passengers could now drink their coffee and eat their soup without it requiring a massive clean-up operation.

"During the course of the tests, there was one amusing incident. My boss, coming to join the test train at Leicester, had left it a little late to arrive there. When crossing the bridge between platforms, he saw a Blue Pullman at a platform, so, without bothering to check the platform number, he dashed down the steps just as the train was starting to pull away. From the window of the test train on the next platform, I saw my boss running along the platform waving his arms and shouting, 'Stop, stop. I want to get on', - this as the service train to London pulled away from him."

But is that all there is to be said? Undoubtedly not and it still does not answer the comments made by staff, that they felt the couplings between the actual vehicles were often too loose, or possibly worked loose through wear, with commensurate effect. Likewise we do not know what other tests may have been conducted to, if not totally negate, at least attempt to reduce the severity of the riding problems. Further discussion on this subject would, though, veer into the speculative arena.

So far as the Midland sets are concerned, we now need to fast forward through to the mid 1960s and the dilemma faced by British Railways themselves relative to the future use of the trains. As is already known, the eventual decision was to base all the sets on the Western Region, although before this there is a definite record of a test run on the Eastern Region to Leeds, with a suggestion that a similar run took place to Harwich.

As can be seen, in addition to the usual Special Traffic Notice that would have been issued, an A4 booklet was printed and distributed to the 'great and the good' who would accompany the outing. They were numerous, those listed being;

British Railways Board	
P. M Shirley	Vice Chairman BRB
J E Nunneley	Chief Passenger Manager BRB
North Eastern Region	
A Dean	General Manager
D S M Barrie	Asst. General Manager (Commercial)
C Birch	Asst. General Manager (Movements)
C Ayers	Passenger Manager
G Brook	Divisional Sales Manager, Leeds
H F Jarvis	Assistant (Electrical Engineering)
E Jones	Marketing Manager
F L Hick	Movements Planning Manager
A W McMurdo	Divisional Manager, Leeds
H Ormiston	Acting CCE
J R Sampson	Movements Operations Manager
J Sinclair	CM & EE
- together with staff concerned.	
Eastern Region	
J R Hammond	General Manager
T C B Miller	Asst. General Manager (Technical)
H W Few	Asst. General Manager (Movements)
J Hancock	Asst. General Manager (Commercial)
C Scutt	CM & EE
R E Evans	CCE
D Hallyburton	Programming Officer
- together with staff concerned.	
Pullman Car Division	
E J Morris	Manager (Pullman Services)

Blue Pullman Test Run

Saturday 16th October 1965

Leeds – King's Cross
King's Cross – Leeds

The actual number of staff traveling is not known, although clearly it must have been a considerable number as there is a note to the effect that, "Senior Officers to join the 3rd vehicle from the front as far as Leeds. Other staff will be accommodated in the 2nd vehicle from the front as from Leeds. Technical staff will be located with their apparatus in the trailing vehicle in the direction of travel". Mr Morris, from the Pullman Car Division appeared to have been representing himself!

As will have been seen from the brochure cover, the train was worked on an out and back turn with Leeds as the start and finish points. The timings were as follows;

Up - referred to as 'Outward'	
Leeds Central, Platform 5	11.22 dep
Doncaster, Eastern Region Officers join	1156. arr 11.57 dep
King's Cross, Platform 7	14.08
Down - referred to as 'Return'	
Kings' Cross, Platform 10	16.05
Doncaster, Eastern Region staff detrain	18.14½ arr 18.17½ dep
Leeds Central, Platform 5	18.54

A more detailed schedule of times and speeds was included for the "Test Run" in both directions, which indicated a speed of 88.5 mph was required at Sandy in the 'up' direction and no less than 89.1 at Newark for the reverse working. This was shown against the usual set maximum of 90 mph. For reasons that are not stated, not necessarily any fault of the train of course, the booked average speed of 71.3 mph in the 'up' direction was not adhered to and arrival at Kings Cross was 1½ minutes late. In the reverse direction there is only a record of the actual run as far as Doncaster, but again this was 1 minute late.

For the benefit of the perhaps not so technical traveling observers, one whole page was devoted to how to calculate speeds by counting the time between quarter mile posts and likewise by counting rail joints.

The booklet also contained details of connecting services available to those traveling from Leeds and Doncaster, also from King's Cross and York as well as that most important of notices that, "Luncheon will be served at 12.30. Tea will be served on the return journey".

Whilst we therefore have detail of the actual run itself, what we do not have are details of the subsequent discussions that must have taken place. Handwritten notes, in the copy of the document from which this information is gleaned, refer to the Blue Pullman set as taking 2 hrs 42½ minutes for the run, which compared favorably with unspecified runs made by D240 and D385, both 2,000 hp diesel (Class 40) locomotives. The schedule also incorporated seven minutes recovery time.

Despite the effort clearly put in to the day, the Eastern Region deemed the riding qualities of the sets to be unsuitable for its use. This is a little surprising and with consideration, may be perhaps the excuse, although certainly not the complete reason the train sets were rejected. Bearing in mind the speed requirements set for the test as well, it was almost as if the ER had specified an impossible task from the outset.

To explain this further we first need to consider who and why this trial run was being undertaken. The answer has to be at the behest of British Railways Board. BRB were keen to see utilization of an expensive investment and the Eastern Region was the obvious place for the sets. The comment on rough riding must, though, be questionable. Eastern Region permanent way was maintained to a very high standard, it had to be, subjected as it was to regular 100+ mph running from the 'Deltic' fleet. Recall also that just over a year later, riding tests with a Southern Region 'Hastings' DEMU set were undertaken on the ER, following the Hither Green disaster of November 1967. The SR unit ran perfectly on ER track. There is no reason why the Blue Pullman should not have done likewise.

It is more likely that the poor ride quality was a smokescreen to cover the same situation which would occur on the Western Region a few years later. Passengers were expected to pay a supplement to travel on the Blue Pullman compared with a faster service available by locomotive hauled, non-supplementary services. Blue Pullman could well be said to have been overtaken by progress quicker than had been anticipated, although in reality this was already anticipated, even when the sets were still on the drawing board.

It has been suggested that a further trail was scheduled to Harwich (presumably from London, Liverpool Street?), although whether this actually took place, or was perhaps even curtailed following the conclusions of the Leeds test, is not known.

But one question still remains concerning why personnel from the North Eastern Region accompanied the trip. The answer to this comes from Charles Long, who comments that at the same time as a Kings Cross - Leeds working was being considered, a further possibility was a Tees-Tyne service, although evidently this would have been of just three cars, the formation being split at some point. All sorts of questions come to light of course, not the least of which is, could a service having seats for just 72 fare paying passengers have been viable? Now we shall never know the answer. (1)

Opposite page, top - *Conversation piece at Snow Hill, 23rd May 1966. The service is the 10.10 am fill-in turn from Paddington, with the red shade displayed over the centre light. It is making ready for the return working. Some years earlier, one of the Blue Pullman sets was on public display at Paddington prior to the start of the service. (The red flash along the side is reflection from the signal at the far end of the platform.)*   *Bill Chapman*

Opposite page, lower - *Uffington, once the junction station for the Farringdon branch, which closed to passengers in 1951 and freight in 1963. The station would remain open until December 1964, although never once did the Pullman service ever call. Last to go was the signal box, in its final years the working haunt of the redoubtable Adrian Vaughan, whose tales of history and signalling in particular are a worthy tribute to a lost era. Despite also being an undoubted steam man, Adrian had time to take this view of an afternoon London bound service from the footbridge. Adrian Vaughan*

The Gas Turbine converted 'Blue Pullman' proposal of 1967 with lightweight 'Budd' bogies.

Regretfully too, no photographic record of the Leeds trial has come to light and relevant comment is conspicuously absent from the contemporary railway journals.

Thus the problem still remained as to the future for the redundant Midland Pullman sets, remembering of course that at this time no final decision had been made that all were to be concentrated on the Western Region.

With the Eastern not interested and no opportunity for further use on the London Midland or Southern, there was almost a radical new approach, which was first mentioned in the April 1867 issue of *Modern Railways*. The magazine carries a photograph of a six-car set and the comment, "It has been suggested that one of these units should be experimentally converted to gas-turbine mechanical traction......". More on this subject is found in the Ian Allan 'Fleet Survey No 6', with the following text accompanying the drawing seen on this page, ".....A little known project of 1966/7 was sponsored by Rolls-Royce Ltd, and had it not been 'stillborn' by fuel costs, it would have probably rescued the 'Blue Pullman' trains. The proposal was to convert them with Dart-engined 1,500 hp gas-turbines, with a single speed mechanical transmission. Considerable weight saving was envisaged, and the trains would have been fitted with lightweight Budd bogies".

But would it have saved the 'Blue Pullmans'? Probably they would have been granted a further lease of life, until the next fuel crisis to hit the western world in 1973. The same article included a further drawing of a next-stage lightweight train, somewhat more streamlined than the Pullmans. It was clear that a 'Blue Pullman' would have been used as a testbed and it hard to see how the comment about rescuing the trains from a early demise would have applied.

Concluding this venture into the realms of 'might have beens', it is worth remembering that two 1,500 hp gas-turbine engines per train would presumably also have taken the place of the auxiliary engines fitted and would have also

have taken over the requirement of providing power for the various secondary train requirements. With a lighter overall weight, and, of course, assuming the ride quality was good on lightweight bogies, there would seem to be no reason why the 90mph service speed might not have been raised to 100 mph. In this way the units may have achieved an increased, although undoubtedly still limited, lifespan.

A final comment from the same issue of 'Modern Railways' referred to the conversion as not likely to take place, as much due to fuel costs as 'WR commercial requirements'.

It would appear that British Railways Board were almost playing Rolls Royce off against the Western Region. Whoever came up first with concrete proposals for the use of the trains could have them. With the WR having now set out a case for running all five sets, the removal of one as a 'test-bed' by Rolls Royce would mean the enhanced WR service would not then be feasible. Of course, had the sets been reformed, as had been one of the intentions at the time, and the Western Region services restricted to a more appropriate level instead of the flood of Pullman trains that operated post 1967, then BRB might have achieved the best of both worlds. It is likely the WR would have been happier as well.

It seems BR were just glad to wash their hands of the whole issue, passing it on to become a regional responsibility, and having someone they could blame if things did not work out. Marylebone missed an opportunity. Rolls Royce had given them a way out, BRB Headquarters were foolish not to take it.

(1) The inside covers of this Supplement reproduce part of the NER Sectional Appendix for April 1966, some months after the test run had taken place. The fact such detail is included on the working of the trains almost implies the NER had either accepted them or been told, 'you are having them'. Yet again a case of research raising more questions than answers. Mush of the detail on operation is also far more than was known of previously.

Received just in time for inclusion, was this remarkable collection of construction views, from the archives of the Historical Model Railway Society and also Roger Carpenter.

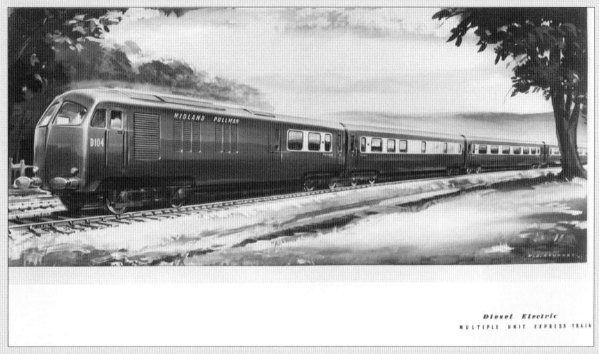

Artists impression from 1957 of the new design, from the hand of P J Ashmore.

Taken from the original book (left), we have a comparison between what was close to the final chosen design and the recently discovered earlier variation. Both by the same artist. Apart from the front end, both sketches are identical but with the aim clearly to present a clean modern impression. Undoubtedly at this stage the major engineering decisions had already been made and here was what almost be regarded as detail, aesthetics of little importance to an engineer, except when it came perhaps to manufacture and maintenance, but vital to the public relations department.

What must be the earlier view on the right, presents a design not unlike that later achieved with the slab front of the 1959 North British Type 2 main line diesel. Whilst half a century later it appears old fashioned and outmoded, bear in mind at the time almost the only main line diesel types in operation were those based on the former LMS and SR concept and external design was very much a step into the unknown.

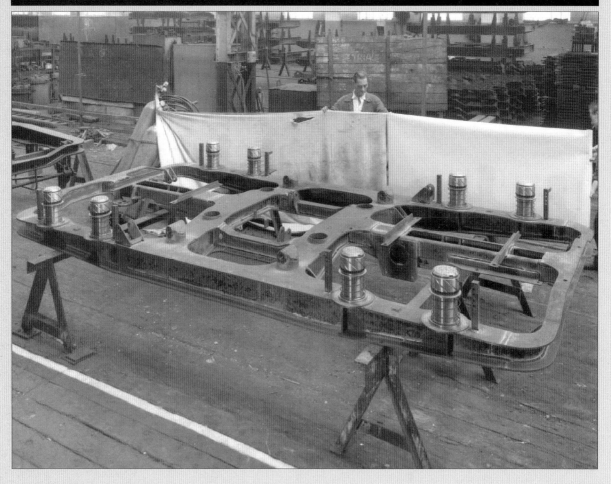

Metro-Schlieren Trailer Bogie framework and spring hangers. An upside down view of the basic structure with pressings and weldings and clearly ready for photographs.

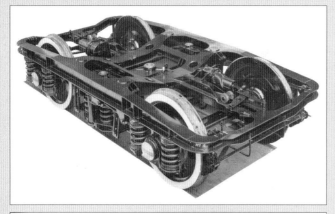

Completed Trailer bogie.

Mike Williams collection

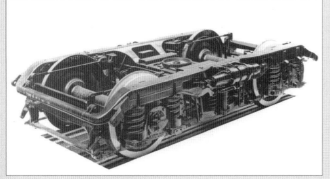

Completed leading bogie from power car.

Mike Williams collection

Top left - First Class Parlour Car Roof.

Top right - The basic roof framework for Parlour Car.

Lower right - Body end being fitted to Parlour Car. In all cases the use of extensive welding can be seen. The views on this page were taken in June 1959.

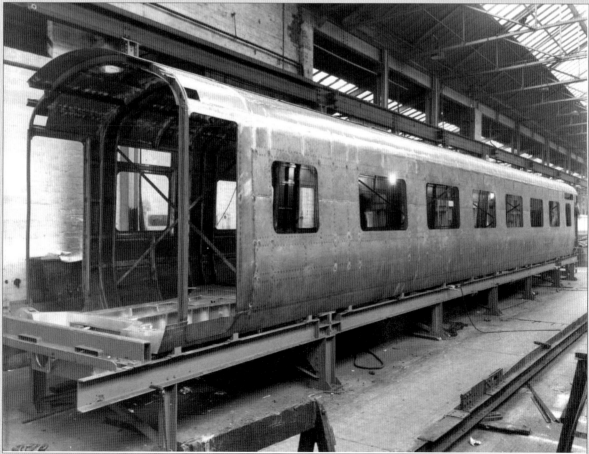

By August / September 1959, work was well under way towards completion of the coach bogies, that shown on this page clearly in the process of painting. (Were any colour views taken of the construction….?)

Opposite top - 1st Class Parlour Car Shell (exterior) - Roof unit being fitted.

Opposite bottom - External three-quarter view of Parlour Car bodyshell with roof, but before ends were fitted

Above - Parlour Car type 6. HO18870 - Half End and Bodyside view. Notice the designation on the end 'Train 1' and presumably referring to what would later become one of the Midland sets.

Right - Pattern of interior panelling. This is believed to be from the interior of an LMR set.

Top left - Motor Car Type p1 (six car train) - Interior View at Passenger Entrance Door.
Top right - Kitchen Car Type 4 (Six car train). View through Kitchen BodySide Doors on Refrigerator & Kitchen Corridor Partition.
Bottom left - Engine Compartment and view of power compartment. In the extreme background two gas cylinders can be seen. They seen rather on the large side for presumably CO2 bottles, could they be fuel for the kitchens?
Bottom right - Completed interior of end compartment of second class parlour car.

Parlour Car type 6. Vestibule End showing Passenger Luggage Compartment and Air Conditioning Control cabinet. Notice the fibreglass insulation to the bodysides.

Motor Car Type P1 (six car train) - Interior View of Driver's Cab, photographed in September 1959.

Amongst other work still be completed are the provision of the folding crew seats. Although recorded by type, aside form the addition of WR ATC, the cab of the WR units was identical.

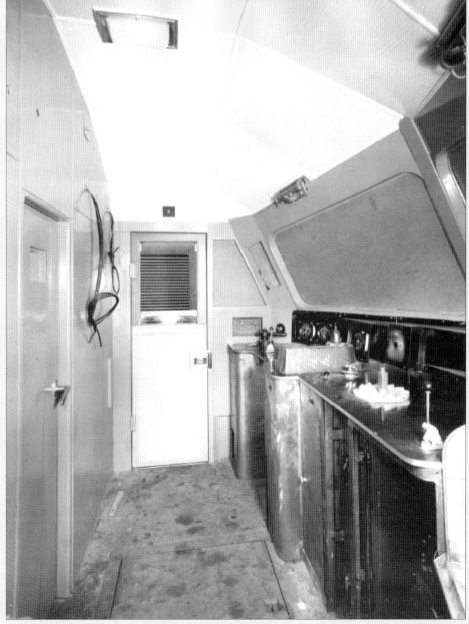

Above - *Believed to be 'Set 1', passing Wembley Hill on the former GCR line with a test run early in 1960.*

Left - *Recorded around the same time, but on this occasion thought to be near Derby. M60093 is leading.*

Left - *Is the colour scheme nanking blue, or could it even be a test outing in works grey? From the presence of the tail lamp this was a view of the rear power car of the train, 1960.*

This page - Mike Williams collection

Right and centre- *A future Midland Pullman 6-car set at Bedford, 11th January 1960. The branch from here to Hitchin was known to have been used for trial running in March 1960 but clearly these two views pre-date that time. The original livery for the kitchen cars will also be noted. It was, of course, altered before the train entered service. By late April 1960 at least one set was based at Cricklewood and running a daily test to an unknown destination, before returning again around 6.10 pm.   D Kingston*

Bottom - *Power Car M60093 at St Pancras after arrival from Manchester. The clock will be noted at 11.03 am, at least 12 minutes ahead of the revised arrival time of 11.15 am. (This arrival time in London had been introduced from January 1961 for two reasons. Firstly to allow the Manchester businessmen more time in London, whilst it also afforded the opportunity for the fill-in afternoon service to be extended to Nottingham, in the hope of attracting additional patronage.) The fact that the crew have already had time to cover the Class 'A' headcode lights and uncover the centre red warning light, implies that the train had been stationary, for a short time at least, prior to the photo being taken. From the condition of the unit, clean but certainly not pristine, this cannot have been a run prior to entering service and the conclusion is reached that this was instead a specially arranged publicity run, where the route had specifically been kept clear. As was mentioned in the original book, this was possible on occasions but it was certainly not practical on a daily basis. The identity of the man shaking hands with the driver and presumably congratulating him on the early arrival, is not reported. There is, of course, a simpler alternative, that the St Pancras station clock was running slow!*
BTC

THE MIDLAND PULLMAN

The classic 'official' view, which was sold as a postcard. (Another, similar coloured view was also available). The location was not given, although from the livery it must certainly be post January 1960. Possibly before the train entered public service.

4th July 1960, 8.50 a.m. and the first day of public service. M60092 leads 'Set 2' (the other vehicles were M60732, M60742, M60743, M60733 and M60093), around the curve at Derby South Junction en-route for London. A special effort was made by the traffic department to ensure there were no hold-ups on the way and indeed the service arrived at St Pancras seven minutes early.

R J Buckley

Leicester North, again on the first day of service, Monday 4th July 1960. According to the photographers notes, "The trains runs forward (from Leicester London Road) to form the 2.33 pm departure to St Pancras". We do not know the results of this first day's Leicester run although, on the return from St Pancras to Manchester Central later that day, it was reported that milepost 40 from London, was passed in 32 minutes, constituting a new record. The set-down time at Cheadle Heath was also eight minutes early. Later in the week, Cheadle Heath was reached four minutes early on both Tuesday and Wednesday and six minutes early on Thursday. There is no mention of Friday, although two months later, in September 1960, it was reported that the new train had put in a "Flawless Performance". Indeed the same comment was made in June 1961, the train running "Commendably". Thus any converse report must be seen in context and not perceived as opportunity to find fault. Indeed the first confirmed report of a difficulty was on 30th October 1961, when a 'Peak' class diesel with five coaches and kitchen car took the place of the up service from Manchester. A similar formation was used for what was then the mid-day Nottingham working. (Officially both sets were home based at Cricklewood, 14A, throughout their time on the LMR, but in practice this did not always mean that the spare set was there. If it were needed, no doubt the proverbial would apply, invariably being at the wrong end of the system!) Notice, in the view above, also the pristine condition of the various underframe components, likewise the interest being displayed by the men at the lineside. Finally, it will be seen that an oil tail lamp is being used, the centre red light covered up. Notwithstanding the inclusion of an electric red lamp on the new trains (covered over in the illustration), it was still BR policy that an oil lamp should be displayed. No doubt this applied on the WR sets as well, although views of the rear of the trains in service are few and far between.

A Swain

new de luxe service

MIDLAND PULLMAN

starts 4 July

Mondays to Fridays inclusive. First Class only

8.50 am	MANCHESTER CENTRAL	9.21 pm
9.04 am	CHEADLE HEATH	9.07 pm
12.03 pm	LONDON ST. PANCRAS	6.10 pm

FIRST CLASS SINGLE FARE 57/6
PULLMAN CAR SUPPLEMENTARY FEE 20/-

Mondays to Fridays inclusive. First Class only

12.45 pm	LONDON ST. PANCRAS	4.00 pm
2.10 pm	LEICESTER LONDON ROAD	2.33 pm

FIRST CLASS SINGLE FARE 31/3
PULLMAN CAR SUPPLEMENTARY FEE 10/-

LONDON MIDLAND

MIDLAND PULLMAN

MANCHESTER—LONDON • LONDON—LEICESTER

These trains are the latest word in luxury, comfort and speed which British Railways now offer. They have been specially designed with the inter-city travel requirements of the modern businessman principally in mind.

The coaches are most distinctive in appearance and the elegant decor of the interiors is restful and relaxing to the traveller. All passenger accommodation is fully air-conditioned. There are roomy individual reclining seats, adjustable at the touch of a small lever.

The windows have double glazing, with venetian blinds between the two panes of glass. There is double insulation against sound and heat, in fact everything possible has been done for the traveller's comfort.

The menus are specially arranged each day and the wine list has been very carefully selected. The food is prepared in kitchens equipped with the most modern appliances.

The staff of the Midland Pullman will do everything they can to add to the pleasure of your journey and to maintain the traditionally high ideals of Pullman service.

As the accommodation is limited to 132 first class seats, intending passengers should always book in advance to make sure of travelling by the Midland Pullman.

Reservations can be made at British Railways stations, offices and official agencies in Manchester, Leicester and London.

The timetable, fares and Pullman supplements are given overleaf.

The front (top left), rear (top right) and centre of a rather bland looking advance publicity handout of 1960. The original is printed with blue ink on white paper, but is certainly not to the standard perhaps expected. The starting date shown was also not that originally intended, this having originally been for January 1960, but then put back for reasons that are not reported. We shall never know if perhaps even at this stage there was some concern over the riding of 'those bogies". Seen here is one of the non powered examples, fitted under the cab of a power car. (In 2008 an original poster for the new service was still present in an abandoned underground tunnel at Euston).

Top - *London bound through Cheadle, 8th July 1965.*

Bottom - *Similarly London bound but this time on the 'fast line' at Chinley North, 20th April 1965.*
Both: John Clarke

The down Manchester service, about to rejoin the main line north of Derby following its detour via the Chaddesden loop, June 1962.

P J Lynch

From the side shadows this is clearly a record of the down evening Manchester service. Recorded near to Kibworth North Signal Box, 16th May 1961.

M Mitchell

From a similar position to that opposite, the down train rejoining the main line north of Derby in June 1962.

P J Lynch

Departure time at St Pancras, 22nd June 1962. The clock records eight minutes after six, the platform already deserted and just two minutes to go. Arrival at Manchester Central was scheduled for 9.21 pm. *'R.C.T.S.' Collection CUL3260*

Pages 34 and 35, Derby Works Open Day, Saturday 15th August 1964. Amongst the stock on display was a freshly overhauled Midland Pullman set including driving cars, M60092, and M60093. Certain of the trailers can also be identified, M60730, M60743 and M60733.

Compared with the formation of 'Set 2', (see lower **caption page 28),** it would appear that at some stage a vehicle swap has occurred between the sets. Whether this was a regular occurrence is not known. Also with only two sets available, it is not known if swaps of the mirror 'half-sets' occurred.

From its pristine external condition, the train would appear almost ready to return to service. The only obvious external difference compared with when built, is the addition of electrification warning flashes.

It would be interesting to know whether the overhaul also included a refurbish of the internal décor as well. Probably 'yes' although no doubt to the same style as previously. Whether the visiting public were permitted to walk through the complete train or were, perhaps more likely, restricted to one small section is uncertain. As the steps are placed against the guard's compartment, the latter is probably the case.

Notice in the lower views the tipped forward position of the driver's seat, necessary due to the restricted space between the rear of the seat and the cab bulkhead. The Metro-Schlieren plate on the bogies will also be noted.

All 'R.C.T.S.' Collection

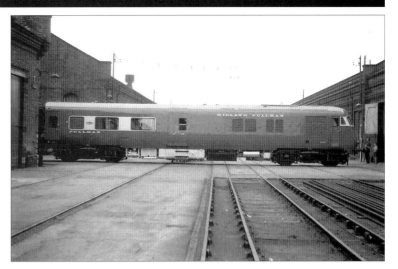

Further Derby Works Open Day views. Specifications for the cars included a wheel diameter of 3' 6" when new, and which was allowed to wear to a minimum 3' 3½". Nowadays we may scoff, but in the 1960s the train crew were advised that if it was desired to use the PA system, the instruction was to switch on and then wait 30 seconds before use - for the valves to warm up. As is known, each table had a call button to summon an attendant, although in practice passengers were reluctant to use these and would instead hail a waiter as he passed.

Both 'R.C.T.S.' Collection

Concluding this section on the LMR is one of Sam Lamberts broadside images, this one of M60740, a Trailer Parlour First. Individually this was the most numerous of any of the specific Blue Pullman vehicles. Ten were built for service in both the LMR and WR trains. (Whilst there were also ten power cars, there were slight regional differences between these.) Although we refer to the trains being built by Metropolitan Cammell at Birmingham, it is important to remember that 'MC' actually occupied four separate works in the area. The sets were assembled at the 'MC' Midland Works, although forgings , and other parts came from Saltney. Old Park Works were responsible for steel pressings. Saltney was also where the drawing offices of the company were located. It has been suggested that a number of full size mock ups of the front end design were also produced.

Whilst the oft quoted trait of the trains is always considered to have been the bogies and ride quality , it should not be forgotten that 'Blue Pullman' had its own legacy in so as far as certain features were concerned. These included the complete close-coupling of a train set, likewise air conditioning and double glazing. All of these were later utilised on the 'HST'. The primary suspension units of the BP Schileren trailer bogies, which according to Malcolm Botham were "reasonably successful", were later chosen by BR for the B4 bogie on the Mk2 coach and supplied by MC under licence to Schileren in large numbers.

Despite the obvious attempt by Metropolitan-Cammell to attract further orders, as witness the invited guest list for the press runs, particularly those on the LMR (see page 32 of the original book), it is not believed there was any serious enquiry from other potential customers.

Further detail has come to light concerning a failure on the down Manchester train that occurred on 27th October 1965. (Certain details are very similar to those ascribed to an event of 27th February 1966 - see page 78 of the original book, although it is assumed that they refer to separate incidents.)

The October 1965 matter concerned the train at Bedford, when the engine of the rear car seized, resulting in what was referred to in the railway press as, "a spectacular mile of skidding with locked wheels and excessive tyre wear". The train was halted at Bedford and "great difficulty was experienced in removing the rear power car"; which was subsequently "dumped" inside Bedford MPD. The remaining five coaches eventually left for Manchester three hours late, with a red tail lamp strung across the last coach; where there was never was any lamp fixing so that it was partly supported with string. Details of the actual power car involved are not recorded for either incident.

Further repercussions were to come as, for whatever reason, the spare Blue Pullman set was not available for the next two days and consequently an emergency arrangement of a 'Peak' hauled scratch set of ordinary stock with a single buffet car was provided. There appears never to have been a time when the LMR and WR borrowed sets from each other.

Operating on the Western Region in what may appropriately be called the first phase of WR operation[1], the new trains quickly settled down into a popular and regular service pattern, seemingly with far fewer complaints about rough riding. As mentioned earlier, part of this easier passage was no doubt due to the better quality of ride on 'Brunels billiard table' as the WR main line was often known. But that is not to say they were absolutely trouble free. As an example, Ray Gomm has fortunately recorded his observations on the Birmingham service during the autumn of 1961, as well as parts of 1962 and through to 1964, and the occasions during this time when the service was replaced by other motive power.

Date	Loco	Train	Note
??-9-1961	6006	Up service	
25-9-1961	6020	Up service	
25-9-1961	7033	Down service	1
26-9-1961	5036		
27-9-1961	6029	Down service	2
29-9-1961	6029	Down service	3
1-12-1961	5043	Up and down workings	4
12-7-1962	D1006	Down service	5
7-1-1963	D1046	Up service	6
2-4-1963	D1004	Up service	7
4-4-1963	7019	Up service	7
11-4-1963	D1006	Up and down workings	
15-8-1963	D1040	Up service	8
2-5-1964	D1690	Up service	

1	4.50 pm ex Paddington
2	11 40 am ex Paddington
3	Mid morning down service
4	Probably mid-day up and down workings
5	12 10 pm ex Paddington
6	1 00 pm ex Wolverhampton
7	Up mid day working
8	Involved in crash at Knowle & Dorridge.

The above should certainly not be taken to imply the WR units were in any way more unreliable and it must also be viewed only as a snapshot, although what is perhaps interesting to analyse is what appears to be two actual complete weeks, in September 1961 and again in April 1964, when, clearly one of the Blue Pullman sets was not available.

The first week was perhaps more unfortunate, as it was only shortly after the Western Region had decided to opt for 100% utilisation of all three sets on weekdays, with the introduction of the diesel hauled 'South Wales Pullman' from the start of the autumn timetable on 11th September 1961.

Whilst the WR may be considered laudable to have attempted such a high utilisation of an expensive asset, the fact that the sets required a regular week out of service for heavier maintenance than could be accommodated at weekends, meant the timing of this so soon after the introduction of the new service was far from ideal. It may well be argued that the new service had to start with the commencement of the new timetable, but it would not really have mattered if, in the interests of reliability, it had started a little later. The use of the 'scratch set' of loco hauled vehicles did little to maintain the credibility of the working to passengers, especially as the Birmingham service was without doubt, far more lucrative than the Bristol train. Assuming, then, the September 1961 loco hauled workings to have been a pre-planned rather than an emergency replacement, this was a badly scheduled interruption. Of course, it might even be asked why, if the Birmingham service was considered more lucrative, did the WR not put the loco hauled train on the Bristol working? This we cannot answer, although there is also the possibility that this, too, may have been affected by 'gremlins' at the same time, or perhaps even there were issues with motive power availability.

Speaking again of the Birmingham Pullman, this time a few years earlier. It was reported in the original book that, as far as the Midland Region was concerned, at least one steam hauled timetable run had taken place in August 1959. The Western Region similarly organised at least one steam special, although

Opposite page - Westbound at Subway Junction, between Royal Oak and Westbourne Park. A WR 8-car set is passing over the 117 yard Subway Tunnel, carrying the main lines over the electrified Hammersmith and City line. The roof detail of the cars is rarely seen in photographs. Although undated, but clearly taken during the summer, the driver would appear to be wearing his uniform issue white coat.

Ian Allan Library

Metro-Cammell Saltney works , 25th June 1960. A new WR 8-car unit receiving attention, probably either prior to or having returned from a test trip. It is believed W60095 is at the head of the set.
R.C.T.S.' Collection CUL3274

this was somewhat earlier, when on 24th October 1957, No 5082 'Swordfish' was noted on what was referred to in *Trains Illustrated* as a 'Pre Pullman Trail'. This was observed passing Princess Risborough at 12.06 in the down direction and then in the reverse direction at High Wycombe at 5.07 pm the same day. It is reasonable to assume also that similar 'test' runs were made for the Bristol and, presumably later, the South Wales services, maybe in each case more than one. But the question must also be asked, were any of these really necessary, or was it partly an excuse for (as Wallis & Grommit might well say), "a grand day out?" Taking the Birmingham test as an example, a two hour service had been operated years previously, indeed as far back as 50 years ago. Some need perhaps, but some fun as well. (2)

Adrian Vaughan also adds a delightful perspective to the operation of the trains in his article in the 1979 *Railway World Annual*, entitled *Signalling the 'Blue Pullmans'*. Whilst it may digress slightly at times from the theme of this book, is well worth reading in itself.

"In the old mechanical boxes you had to be nimble to keep the Pullman's road clear.

"The Metro-Cammell 'Blue Pullman' diesel multiple-units made their debut on the London Midland Region in 1939." (Undoubtedly a 'typo', as even 1959 was incorrect as it should have read 1960 of course.) "The following year three eight-car sets were handed over to the Western Region, which soon started Birmingham and Bristol Pullman services from London. In 1961 a Paddington - South Wales service was added. The 'Bristol Pullman' and 'South Wales Pullman' I saw almost weekday in and weekday out, for I was a signalman at Challow or later Uffington throughout their careers.

"The 'Bristol Pullman' worked to this weekday schedule:
08.15 Bristol-Paddington
11.45 Paddington-Weston-super-Mare
 2.50 Weston-super-Mare-Paddington
 5.45 Paddington-Bristol

"The 'Swansea Pullman' started for Paddington at 6.50 and returned from London at 4.40, but in 1964 they decided the set could not be left idle midday. So a shuttle service was arranged like this:
 6.50 Swansea-Paddington
11.00 Paddington-Cardiff
 2.30 Cardiff-Paddington
 5.40 Paddington-Swansea

"To signalmen in 1961 the 'Blue Pullmans' looked exceptionally fast. We credited them with speeds of l00 mph between

The opposite end of the same set in the course of shunting. The fact that a tail lamp is attached might well imply a test on BR metals. This time it is believed the power car is W60094.

R.C.T.S.' Collection CUL3265

Badminton and Wootton Bassett, taking their point-to-point running times as a guide, but remember that in 1961 we were still unused to diesel pace, which was unquestionably faster than that of the average steam engine we saw. By 1964 Pullman speed was no longer remarkable.

"Up to 1958 steam-hauled express trains still ran the 77.5 miles between Swindon and Paddington (or vice versa) on schedules varying from 71min for the 'Bristolian' to 89 min for the 'Red Dragon'. With the complete takeover of express trains by diesels in the autumn of 1963, variations of non-stop - and even start-to-stop - schedules became minimal. All trains ran very fast whether they had the dignity of a nameboard or not. These were some typical Swindon-Paddington and Paddington-Swindon schedules in early 1964:

"The 11.15 Bristol and 11.00 Paddington called at Swindon. The 4.55

Up	min	Down	min
'Bristol Pullman'	75½	'Bristolian'	72
'Swansea Pullman'	70½	09.00 Paddington	72
'Red Dragon'	74½	11.00 Paddington	73
11.15 Bristol	76	4.55 Paddington	73
'Bristolian'	75½	'Bristol Pullman'	71

Paddington was the 'Cheltenham Spa Express'. This and the South Wales expresses were 'Western' diesel-hauled while Bristol trains, apart from the Pullman, were 'Warship'-hauled.

"The 'Blue Pullmans' were by no means the first trains to run at such speeds. Between 1932 and 1939 the 14.40 from Cheltenham, the 'Cheltenham Flyer', covered the 77.3 miles in 65 min start to stop, the 'Bristolian' in 63 min up and 66 min down; a few others made the run in 72-75 min pass to stop. As far back as 1910 two up trains were allowed 74 min from passing Swindon to the Paddington stop.

"The 'Bristol Pullman' was the first regular Pullman working into Temple Meads station, but not the first west of Reading. In the summer of 1955 a train of traditional Pullman coaches was introduced between Paddington and Swansea, leaving London behind a 'Castle' each morning at 08.50 and returning from Swansea at 16.30 (there was a far earlier Pullman service out of Paddington, the short-lived 'Torquay Pullman' of 1929). The diesel Pullmans were originally painted blue below window level, white from the windows to the roof. Emblazoned across the front of the blue, bullet nose of each power car was the Pullman coat of arms, very flamboyantly done in red and gold. Red buffer stocks set off the blue fronts very nicely - looking back on them they really

A WR set on a pre-service trial entering Gloucester (Midland) on 3rd February 1960. Clearly sometime between the 11th January (see views on page 27) and this date, the revised livery for the kitchen cars had been decided upon. P J Sharpe

Pre-service WR publicity photograph taken on the down relief west of Reading in May 1960. A comparison with several of the other photographs reveals the original underframe colours of black and silver / aluminium, quickly faded to a grey / black after a short time of running.

were quite handsome trains. The driver wore a blue-and-white uniform - to be promptly dubbed 'the Wall's Ice-cream man' - and I believe each unit carried one or two fitters to keep the engines running nicely. In their final years the Pullmans were repainted in BR's Pullman livery with blue around the windows and pearl-grey over the rest of the bodywork.

"The timekeeping of the Pullman services was quite good. On 13 weekdays between 11 May and 28 May 1965 I recorded the 08.15 Bristol as passing Uffington 4min early, 1 min early, right time, 2 min late on six occasions, and on the remaining days 3, 4, 5 and 6 min late. The 06.50 Swansea, which followed 10 min behind the 'Bristol Pullman' was, over the same period 2 min early twice, right time twice, 2 min late on five occasions, and 3, 7, 8 and 12 min late on the remainder.

"To signal the Pullmans from box to box the old Great Western Railway bell code 4-1-3 'Is Line Clear for Express Diesel Railcar?' was revived. On the down line at Challow, before 'Line Clear' could be acknowledged to Wantage Road for a Pullman, 'Line Clear' had to be obtained from Uffington. This was a special instruction applying only to the diesel Pullmans because the authorities felt that the down distant signal at Challow was not far enough away from the first 'stop' signal to provide sufficient braking distance for such fast trains. Yet, as can be seen from the tables, they were not that much faster than regular, locomotive-hauled trains. The 'Warship'-hauled 'Bristolian' was just as fast, but in 1964 no special instructions were in force for it at Challow. Curiously enough, the precautions adopted for the Pullman trains had been ordered for the 'Bristolian' when it first went over to diesel haulage, but they were later found unnecessary and so they were dropped.

"Such special precautions led signalmen over the years to believe that diesels had inferior brakes to steam engines. Men who had signalled the 'Cheltenham Flyer' before the war remembered that no special precautions were thought necessary to ensure its braking distance; and that train was the fastest the route saw until the introduction of the HST in 1975.

"After the 4.40 Paddington had been re-timed to 5.40, the 'long-block' section working at Challow sometimes caused delay, because the two trains ran down from London at such close headway. Quite frequently only 4 min separated them at Steventon. While this was tolerable on lines signalled with four-aspect colour-lights, it was a chronic problem on semaphore-signalled lines, where the boxes were almost too far apart

for such very close running.

"Consider, for instance, the working of the 5.40 and 5.45 Paddington Pullmans on 13 May 1965. The 5.40 cleared Challow at 6.07 as the 5.45 was passing Steventon. Challow sent 'Train out of section' to Wantage Road for the 5.40, but had to 'refuse' the 5.45 until the 5.40 had cleared Uffington. At 5.49 Uffington sent 'TOS' for the 5.40 and the signalman rapidly rattled out 4-1-3 to Uffington for the 5.45, Uffington acknowledged it and turned the indicator to 'Line Clear'. Challow then tapped out 4-1-3 to Wantage Road and turned the indicator to 'Line Clear', thus releasing Wantage Road's intermediate block signals at Circourt, But the 5.45 was by then passing Wantage at 90mph, The yellow gleam of the IB distant signal was reflected on the sides of the coaches, changing to green just as the driver was about to shut off power; we had 'given him the distant' with a second to spare!

"There had been a frantic tapping of bells and walloping of heavy levers by three signalmen 6½ miles apart but all working in perfect unison, knowing exactly what was happening at the other boxes. Such close working was not really good railway practice, but we certainly enjoyed the challenge of trying to squeeze a quart into a pint pot. All of us were well pleased to know that we had got away with it again.

"The time-keeping of the 5.45 shows how well the semaphore system coped with 'the impossible'. During the 14 weekdays from 11 May to 28th May 1965, the train was respectively 11 min late passing Uffington, 5 min late, right time, 2 min early twice, 3 min early on five occasions, 4 min early, 7 min early, 8 min early and 11 min early. The last occasion was on 21 May, when the 4.45 had managed to get away from Paddington in front of the 5.40 and to celebrate the driver had picked up all his recovery time so that he passed Uffington, 66½ miles out from Paddington, in 53 min - which, if I may draw tedious comparisons, was almost as fast as the epic run of the 'Castle'-hauled 5.00 from Paddington on 6th June 1932.

"A curious side-effect of the introduction of diesel traction was that some signalmen, myself included, tended to say to themselves 'they'll make it up' when they were obliged to check an express. We never thought that in steam days, when we knew each minute gained on schedule had been paid for by a hard-working fireman. I remember a signalman who had been unable to get his signals 'off quickly enough for the 'Castle'-hauled 'Bristolian', which therefore got a distant signal check and lost at

The Birmingham service passing Old Oak Common on the last stage of its journey. The earlier comment concerning the discolouration of the underframe components is noticeable. R H G Simpson

Above - *Platforms 5 and 6 at Paddington with two sets awaiting departure. The irregular positioning of the car numbers does little to assist identification, 13th July 1961.   R.C.T.S.' Collection CUL3278*
Opposite top - *Departure from Paddington, but probably for servicing. For this move it was practice for one driver to be in the cab at either end,13th July 1961. Note also that by this time, authority had been given to dispense with an oil tail lamp.   R.C.T.S.' Collection CUL3279*
Opposite centre - *A particularly interesting view showing a set being cleaned between workings in the sidings opposite to Royal Oak. This would have no doubt have been either just before or subsequent to the mid-day fill in turn.   R.C.T.S.' Collection WARD255*
Opposite bottom - *W60648, a parlour second. The second class Pullman vehicles had a silver surround to the window, compared with a gold surround for first class. Only a single window blind was fitted. In both first and second class vehicles, the blinds had a tendency to rattle between the double glazed windows.   R H G Simpson*

Above - *London bound. The 'Bristol Pullman' (or should it the 'London Pullman' as the train is heading east!?), leaving Box Middle Hill tunnel. At a length of 216 yards, the tunnel was not all that much longer than that of the train, 175 yards. For the 1964 timetable only, the mid-day fill in turn was extended from Bristol through to Weston-super-Mare, although the need for a rapid turn-around meant few, if any, passengers travelled in both directions on the same day. This compared with the three hours available to passengers on the later Oxford working although, as with the extension to Weston, neither was considered a commercial success.*

Left - *This time the Bristol bound service is not far from its destination. It is seen passing through St Anne's Park station and with Bristol No 2 tunnel in the background. Immediately to the right of the power car is the famous 'apple and pear'. Two chunks of sandstone excavated from the tunnel during construction. They were subsequently donated by British Railways to Bristol University.*

Both; George Heiron / The Transport Treasury

least 5 min running time. The signalman was nearly in tears. He rushed to his window, trying to look apologetic and simultaneously to wave 'right away' to the driver so as to prevent the man creeping on from signal to signal until he was convinced that they were all 'off. The engine whistle shrieked and a great column of smoke erupted from the copper-capped chimney as the coasting 'Castle' was opened up to regain the earlier 95 mph. Looking down from the box one had an excellent view on to the footplate - the glorious fire, the polished metal. This time all we saw was the driver waving his watch and the fireman swinging his shovel. When the diesels came on the scene we weren't nearly so worried about 'knocking five minutes out of the fast' - in fact, we coined a new phrase. 'Give 'em a tickle', we used to say.

"This new attitude, combined with an enthusiastic signalman's desire to run as many trains as possible 'main line', developed a splendid game with the morning Pullmans on occasions.

"On any weekday up to late 1962 Challow box was a busy place between 9.00 and 9.30, particularly on the up road. First, the 7.05 Cheltenham to Paddington express, 'Castle'-hauled, called to pick up passengers. This was followed by the 12.05 am Tavistock Junction to Banbury express freight, hauled by a 59XX 'Hall' and usually known as the 'Tavi'. Behind it sped both diesel Pullmans. The Cheltenham had to be diverted from up main to up relief line in order to call at Challow station platform. Its driver always worked his 'Castle' hard away from the Challow stop on to the main line because he knew that the 'Bristol Pullman' was only 10 or 12 min behind. The 'Tavi' had to go up relief line to Wantage, although it was a very fast-running train, because of the Cheltenham 'pulling out in front', so to speak, and the Pullmans coming up fast behind. If the 'Bristol Pullman' were 3 or 4 min late it was possible to take a chance and let the goods run up the main, but it usually came up from Uffington so fast that the Cheltenham had not cleared my intermediate block signals at Circourt. Usually, therefore, I had not been able to clear my up distant so the goods had to brake, thereby losing valuable time and forcing me to 'put it away'. This was annoying for me and for the driver of the 'Tavi', who often did not understand why he had been delayed. I loved to see a steam engine tearing along. If only the 'Tavi' would take about 45 sec longer to reach my up distant, I could clear it and give the freight a run. But I needed the driver's co-operation for this.

"My opportunity came one Monday morning. The 'Tavi', running at nearly 60mph behind No 5945, passed my distant at caution as usual and came crawling round the bend to find the signals off for the up relief line. The driver stopped his train in the platform and came on the phone to ask why the Tavi', one of the fastest trains of the day, always 'got put in' at Challow. At last I had a chance to explain the situation and ask if he would give my theory a trial, to which he readily agreed. Next day the Cheltenham was about right time and the 'Bristol Pullman' was 4min late - perfect conditions for the experiment. As the 'Tavi' passed Uffington my mate there sent the 'Train entering Section' bell, then rang me on the phone. That up one was running very well, but they shut off passing here', he said wonderingly in his gentle Welsh accent. Just what we want, I thought. The Cheltenham was blazing away towards Circourt signals and would clear them in another 2½min. I waited for the buzzer which sounded when a train passed the Circourt signals, then sent the 'Train entering Section' to Wantage Road and whipped over my up main signal levers, the final one clearing the distant.

"To use footplate slang, 'it dropped down the chimney' of No 5945. There was the lovely sound of an appreciative far-off whistle, then the urgent beat of an engine being worked up hard from about 35mph. Each speed seemed to produce different rhythms - and beautiful they were. No 5945 came pounding up towards the box, whistle screaming and the footplate men waving. They would be running at 60 mph by the time they passed Circourt, 35 wagons rattling and swaying behind. The driver went so well that he cleared from the main line to the West Curve at Foxhall without delaying the Bristol, though it was a very close-run thing at Steventon! The return working for the Swindon men on the 'Tavi' was with the 3.00 Croes Newydd, steel plate for Pressed Steel-Fisher at Swindon. I was able to tell them, as they passed the box, that the gamble had paid off. After that the word spread and we often found it possible, using the understanding between drivers and signalmen, to run the 'Tavi' in front of both Pullmans.

"The Pullman services had their fair share of traction failures and other mishaps. We were not properly hardened to diesel failures (BR issued instructions to station announcers that in apologising to passengers for delays the term 'diesel failure' must never be used, only 'locomotive failure') and the apparent frailty of these powerful, thermally efficient monsters was then something of a marvel. On several occasions the diesel Pullman on one route or another had to be taken out of service and replaced by a diesel locomotive and eight traditional Pullman coaches. This happened on 14th January 1964, when the 6.50 Swansea was put out of action by a fire in one power car. The engine burst into flames as the train was leaving Swansea and the passengers were transferred to the 7.20. After attention the 6.50 left 'light' for Paddington, but the flames erupted again at Bridgend and the unit had to be taken out of service, so the stand-by coaches had to make a quick dash to Paddington for the return working that day. In June that year the stand-by coaches were again in use on the 8.15 Bristol, hauled by a D10XX diesel. On 15th June the 'Western' diesel on the standby train itself failed at Didcot. The diesel was taken off and its crew took over the station pilot, 'Hall' No 6937, for the 53 miles on to Paddington. They had eight Pullman cars weighing about 350 tons and a fire rather on the low side, so the start from Didcot was very gentle until the fireman had got matters in hand. They passed Goring at 75 mph and were all set to make up a few minutes on the schedule when they were checked at Reading owing to the 6.20 Newton Abbot-Paddington dragging away from the station. But the Newton must then have run well, for No 6937 was able to make a steady 80 after Maidenhead and got to Paddington in 33 min from Reading. Without the check she would have made it in the even half-hour, but as it was she improved on the diesel Pullman time by 2 min.

"The vulnerability of the diesel Pullman was demonstrated one day at Challow in 1962 when a brake block fell off and ripped open the fuel tanks. The train stopped at the signalbox while the fitters fitted handkerchiefs into the gaping rents and after some banter from the signalman on the advisability of summoning *City of Truro* from Didcot to give them a shove the Pullman trundled off to Swindon. Parts of the transmission used to fall off occasionally too.

"One such incident happened at about 6.15 on 8th January 1963. The driver of the 4.03

The route taken by the Bristol Pullman varied between that via Bath and that via Badminton, according to the year in question as well as the time of day. (See original book for further details.) The South Wales Pullman always took the Badminton route, hence it is not always easy to identify which service was being recorded. This particular view is believed to be latter, judging from the number of words on the destination panel to the side of the power car. The scene was as the train was passing Westerleigh East Signal Box, 106 miles from Paddington and the junction with the north east connection to the LMR route between Bristol and Gloucester.

George Heiron / The Transport Treasury

Old Oak Common freight, with a 92xxx 2-10-0, was used to running his train very fast between Didcot and Swindon to get through without being sidetracked for any express trains. His engine took water on the loop at Highworth Junction and was then 'turned out' behind the 4.40 Paddington, the 'Swansea Pullman'. He was running very well, but was surprised to be brought to a stand by signals at Little Somerford. How fast had he been running, he wondered, to catch up the Pullman? He needn't have worried: the Pullman had failed at Hullavington, strewing so much of its innards along the track that its crew thought they had smashed into a motor car.

"Not every delay was due to faulty mechanism. On or about (as the policeman says in court) 25th July 1963 the 5.45 Paddington was close to Maidenhead when it hit a dog - quite a large dog, in fact. The impact shattered the compressed air pipes at the front

of the train, putting the front engine out of action. The train limped on (the dog could not, it was dead) into Reading, during which time Control had decided that the train must be taken out of service there and its passenger torn from their dinners and put on to the 6.45 Paddington to Bristol, which was stopped specially to pick them up. But Control had forgotten it was Friday and most long-distance trains out of Paddington were crowded. The 6.45 duly came to a stand at the platform, but the scores of 5.45 passengers could hardly get in the doors. They were repulsed, as you might say, with heavy losses. Persuaded of the impossibility of getting any more on to the 6.45, Control allowed it to go on. The Pullman was brought back from the sidings, its passengers were reunited with their cold dinners and off they went to Bristol, arriving there some 3hr late.

"There was an ambition among the signalmen at Wantage Road and Challow to

Above - *Into the afternoon sun and down one of the long 1 - 300 gradients between Chipping Sodbury and Coalpit Heath. The train is shortly to pass under one of several aqueducts on this section of line, intended to relieve pressure on the water course and reduce the risk of the railway flooding. This has not always been totally effective and the line, around Chipping Sodbury in particular, has been under water on a number of occasions over the years.*

Left - *Speeding west, again on the Badminton line and, according to the photographer's record, at Chipping Sodbury. With the disused double junction in the background, perhaps Wapley may be more likely.*

Both; George Heiron / The Transport Treasury

route any of the Pullmans along the relief lines. This we contrived to do once in a while. I managed it when the down main line was blocked by an ex-LMS 2-8-0 which had a broken spring over its trailing driving wheels and again when I had a points failure. But the credit for the finest piece of trickery ever perpetrated on a Pullman must go to a colleague of mine at Challow. At the time it seemed to be a stunning improvisation to keep traffic moving, but in retrospect I have a feeling it was horribly illegal. The 6.01 Didcot to Swindon stopping train was scheduled to wait at Challow to allow both 5.40 and 5.45 Paddington Pullmans to pass. On this evening the 5.40 coasted to a stand at Challow and asked for assistance because the engines had failed. Locomotives may have been available at Didcot or Swindon, but my mate wasn't going to lose this opportunity of 'getting one over' the Pullman. He suggested that the

down stopper should get on the front of the Pullman and tow it to Swindon. The Pullman train crew agreed, but I don't know if anyone asked Control (we rarely did ask them; we usually told them after the event). The stopper consisted of 2-6-2T No 6136 and two coaches, which were duly backed on to the Pullman and coupled up. Not being a locomotive man I cannot say for certain, but I don't think that the vacuum brake operated by the driver on No 6136 could be coupled to the Pullman, in which case the extra eight cars were taken to Swindon on the brakes of the steam engine and its two coaches alone, which would have been a sin against every rulebook imaginable. Anyhow, the most unusual train the line had seen for a very long time set off at a cracking pace amidst much derisive whistling from No 6136 and sarcastic cheering from porters and signalman. We split our sides wondering what the Pullman passengers made of the strange whistles and chuffs coming from the front end and why they kept stopping at tiny little stations and wooden halts."

Perhaps an even more appropriate title might have been, "Getting one over on the Pullmans".

(1) - 'Part 1' might conveniently be called the days up to the end of 1966, when the services were operated by the original three eight car trains. 'Part 2' would then refer to the final years with all five sets concentrated on the Western Region.

(2) 'Trains Illustrated' - December 1957. "In connection with the forthcoming introduction of diesel multiple-unit Pullmans on the Birmingham line, a high speed trial with a "Castle", a five-coach set of B.R. standard stock and a track-testing car (presumably the 'white-wash coach') was carried out between Paddington and Wolverhampton on October 24. No. 5082 was the engine and a 110-min. schedule was laid down to Birmingham and 135 min. to Wolverhampton. Leaving Paddington at 11.30 a.m., No. 5082 was through Princes Risborough (34.6 miles) at 12.06, 5 min. early.

Only 19 min. were taken over the 22.6 miles on to Ardley, but this was 1½ min. more than the schedule ordained, and at Banbury, passed at 12.40, the special was reported 1½ min. down, having lost 5 min. on the 10-min. booking from Ardley to Banbury for reasons of which we are not aware, but which doubtless had to do with the engineering works in the Banbury area. The deficit had increased to 2 min. by Leamington, passed at 12.58, and Birmingham was reached 1 min. late at 1.21. On the return journey, however, No. 5082 sprinted up from Birmingham to Paddington in 107 min. to arrive 5 min. early. Leaving Snow Hill at 3.45, No. 5082 had 2½ min. in hand as early as Leamington (23.3 miles), which was passed in 21 min. and although some of the gain was once more lost in the Banbury area, the "Castle" was still ½ min. up at Ardley, passed at 4.38; the 53.4 miles to this point had been run in 53 min. Point-to-point times thereafter were exactly maintained to High Wycombe, Ashendon (66.5 miles) being passed in 64 min. at 4.49, Princes Risborough (75.9 miles) in 73 min. at 4.58 and High Wycombe (84 miles) in 82 min. at 5.07. The finish, one guesses, was a blaze of fireworks downhill to Denham, for the 18.8 miles from High Wycombe to Greenford were reeled off in 14 min. at an average of 80 m.p.h., so that the special was into Paddington at 5.32."

Above - *The 7.00 a.m. up Birmingham Pullman passing West Ruislip, 21st September 1963. The excuse, if one were needed, for including the view has to be the presence of the steam engine alongside. Obviously not the same circumstances as those described by Adrian Vaughan, but a reasonable link nonetheless. The white covers on two of the three air horns are an interesting addition.* Ian Allan Library

Left - *In the Bristol suburbs. One final recollection of the sets in the Bristol area comes form a former signalman. "During my time at Dr Days, the Blue Pullman was stored overnight in the sidings. I remember coming to work at 6.00 am to see the set derailed on the catch points protecting the relief road. Overnight the Pullman had developed a fault in one of its cabs and the decision was made to turn the set around so the good cab faced London. What should have happened was that the train would reverse out of the sidings on to the down main towards Lawrence Hill. Then, with the good cab, drive around the loop onto the London line and reverse into Temple Meads. Easy - yes. In fact - no. In the sidings, the driver was at the far end and relying on the shunter to give him a hand signal to set back. The shunter always said he received a hand signal from the signalman. The signalman denied it, saying why should he give a hand signal, when there is a dummy on the ground to tell the shunter when the road was set? The long and short of it was the catch point's worked admirably and by 9.00 am the box was full of 'suits'.........2.00 pm could not come around quick enough."* George Heiron / The Transport Treasury

'The Birmingham Pullman'. *Undoubtedly the flagship service so far as the Western Region was concerned, the provision of the luxury service was in many ways a 'sop' to the business travellers of England's second city. At this time planned disruption was to take place, because of the electrification of the line from Euston. The fact that the service was aimed only at the higher echelons of business travel was an irrelevance, lesser mortals having to put up with the disruption. (Where have we heard that one before?)*

Above - *The same service as depicted overleaf, the 7.00 Wolverhampton Low Level to Paddington, restarting south from the Solihull stop, 21st June 1961. The gestured tea cup offering from the second man will be noted.*

Michael Mensing

Opposite top - *From the shadows, this must be the up afternoon service, at Leamington Spa. It would be interesting to know the loadings for the mid-day turns, but they must have been reasonable as they remained a feature of the train working until 1966.*

P J Sharpe

Opposite lower - *The down afternoon Paddington - Wolverhampton Low Level Pullman service leaving Solihull and passing a goods yard, clearly no longer in its prime. This service departed from Paddington at 4.50 pm and was due at Birmingham Snow Hill at 6.55 pm. Journey time to Wolverhampton was a further 25 minutes.*

Michael Mensing

Platform 5 Birmingham Snow Hill, 31st January 1961, probably just after 2.00 pm. This was the platform used by Paddington arrivals. The fact the headlights are covered, indicates this was the 12.10 pm from London and which will return from the same platform at 2.20 pm.

'R.C.T.S.' Collection PMB0102

Just over three weeks later, on 23rd February, another set is ready to perform the same return working, with tail lamp now fitted. First, though, it will have to await the passing of a down freight, seen climbing out of the tunnel behind 2-6-2T No 5184.

Michael Mensing

Driving trailer motor brake seconds at Birmingham Snow Hill. The top and bottom views were taken on 31st January 1961 and that in the centre on 10th May 1961. Unfortunately only the power car in the centre can be positively identified, as W60094. Unlike their LMR counterparts, the WR power cars, were not provided with lavatory accommodation.

R.C.T.S.' Collections; top - PMB0101, centre - CUL3267, lower - PMB0103.

Above - *First Class Parlour Car No W60745. The grill above the lavatory window was for ventilation. Birmingham Snow Hill, 10th May 1961.*

R.C.T.S.' Collection CUL 3271

Above - *Motor Parlour Second (non-driving) No W60645. The bogie differences will be noted.*

R.C.T.S.' Collection CUL 3273

Opposite top - *The opposite end of the type of vehicle above, this is W60644.*

R.C.T.S.' Collection CUL 3268

Opposite centre - *Trailer Kitchen First, W60734.*   *R.C.T.S.' Collection CUL 3269*

Opposite lower - *Within the same eight car unit was W60735, another Trailer Kitchen First W60735.*

R.C.T.S.' Collection CUL 3272

All recorded at Birmingham Snow Hill, 10th May 1961.

The Midland and Birmingham Pullman ceased operation from 18th April 1966 and 3rd March 1967 respectively, Pullman passengers for both Birmingham and Manchester now travelling from Euston. So far as both the former routes traversed by the Blue Pullman sets were concerned, that from St Pancras reverted to loco hauled main line workings, it would not be until a cascade of HST sets appeared decades later that anything like the luxury of service was again available; although now for the masses rather than a select few.

Likewise, the former WR Birmingham main line fared badly. Downgraded and singled in places, there was even threat of one time of closure between High Wycombe and Banbury although since privatisation a resurgence has occurred and through services again run to Birmingham although this time from Marylebone and with journey times broadly similar to what was being achieved 40 years earlier although now with considerably more stops.

We know little of the fate of the two six-car Midland Pullman sets between April and July 1966. Presumably they were in store, but where is not certain. It is believed their actual transfer, both on paper and likewise in the flesh (perhaps that should be the metal and plastic), to the Western Region took place sometime prior to July 1966. Certainly in November 1966 one of the trains was recorded passing Newbury on a crew training run. (- see illustration on page 123 of the original book.)

By this time also, the former Midland Pullman Pullman set referred to above had also received a yellow from end, the first step in removing the individual Pullman identity of the trains, as the Pullman crest formerly on the front of the cars was not restored. It is also difficult to determine exactly when yellow ends were similarly painted on the remaining four units, although it is almost certain neither of the Midland Pullman sets were running out of St Pancras with this adornment. Sometime also between November 1966 and March 1967, work was undertaken to fir the two 6-car sets for multiple-unit running, presumably at Swindon.

Arguably the final and most devastating change was the overall substitution of the blue and white livery for that of a bland grey and blue. As has been commented elsewhere, it was a choice far from ideal for the sets and which also weathered to a shabby appearance within days. No amount of washing would restore the pristine appearance either. Mostly this change appears to have taken place from 1968, although a study of photograph dates, reveal the former WR 8-car sets were so treated first. Indeed, apart from their repainted front ends, the 6-car trains were still resplendent in their original livery as late as 1969.

In the same year, 1969, the Western Region, as is known, approached BRB proposing the withdrawal if the sets. This was vetoed by Marylebone on the basis that as yet there was nothing to replace them - 'HST' was still some seven years in the future. Instead Paddington were advised to 'reduce maintenance', and which immediately implies that the revenue being accrued had also reduced. Surprisingly to report, this was the same year in which the former Midland Pullman units were then fully repainted! Possibly even Paddington had hoped to avoid the expense of a repaint if approval had been given to withdrawal. From this time on then, set swaps, particularly amongst the power cars appears to have taken place although as set numbers were never provided it is difficult, if not impossible to compose a record of these changes.

Variations in front end colours, Opposite top - The original colours as portrayed on a westbound set passing through Swindon. Throughout the life of the sets on the WR, overhauls were undertaken at Swindon. No doubt this applied to all five sets from late 1966 onwards. At some stage, it was reported that six rolls of carpet destined for the trains had vanished from the works, similarly a quantity of paint intended for the trains. None was ever recovered, despite the police having their suspicions and checking several houses. The carpet was well hidden and one house, it was reported to be in Wootton Bassett, was eventually carpeted throughout!

John Metters

Opposite lower - With the body sides still in overall blue, but with a bland yellow end devoid of the Pullman crest / coat of arms. For the present the crest was still present on the bodysides, located mid way between the last two windows of each vehicle. During repainting, the crest was not restored, leaving just the word 'Pullman' on the bodysides.

George Heiron / The Transport Treasury

Derek Everson was employed as an Electrical Fitter at Old Oak from June 1968 onwards and fortunately recorded several views of the sets, in both black and white and colour from 1966 onwards. Opposite are two views of M60092, a former Midland Pullman Motor Brake First. The same vehicle, but with a clearer idea of the style of painting applied to the side, is seen in the lower view.

On this page is a pair of views of the opposite end of the same set, M60093 is shown in both. (This is the same set formation as the original LMR 'Set 2 - see page 28). On M60093, the yellow front end has been applied far more vigorously and is in the style that was later adopted. The conclusion must be that the Swindon were experimenting, although it is known that M60090 also received the same style as seen on page 62, in July 1966.

Notice also that for the present the word 'Midland' was retained on the side. This was later painted out in a rather crude fashion, which remained obvious for as long as the cars retained their blue livery. By December 1967, at the latest, the former LMR vehicles had also all had their 'M' prefix replaced by a 'W', although the same numbers were retained.

At this stage, it will be noted that connections for the multiple operation had yet to be added. The views were taken at Old Oak Common on 8th November 1966.

63

Above - 9th May 1969, and what is now W60092, a former Midland Pullman power car, reposes outside the front of what is still known as the Pullman shed at Old Oak Common. The ex Midland sets were never fitted with roller blind destinations, as were the WR power cars, and a hanging destination board was provided instead during their time on the WR.

A Swain

Below - With three covers over the air horns, an unidentified ex Midland Pullman unit awaits departure from Bristol Temple Meads with the 12-car up 'Bristol Pullman, 5th June 1968.

Colin Maggs

Above - The mid-day six car formation leaving Bristol Temple Meads for Paddington, 20th December 1967. It is all too obvious where the word 'Midland' has been obliterated. Interestingly, it does not appear that any class differential has been added to the doors, in which case a cunning passenger could well avail themselves of first class accommodation for a second class fare!   *P J Fowler*

Below - The tail end of a Paddington service, passing through the distinctive Sydney Gardens, at Bath, 4th October 1968.   *C L Caddy*

Above - *The morning down Pullman service, emerges into the daylight from St Anne's Park No 2 tunnel, 26th September 1967. At this point the train has less than two miles to run to its destination. Notice that the three air horns of this unidentified ex Midland power car are now grouped together on one side of the draw hook whilst covers, or baffles, have not been fitted.*

P J Fowler

Opposite top - *At the same location, but this time some 18 months later, 1st April 1969, another unidentified set emerges into daylight, this time with covers over the horns. The spear fencing and cast iron notices afford reflection to an earlier era.*

P J Fowler

Opposite lower - *August 22nd 1968, with the 'South Wales Pullman' service recorded at Newport.*
John H Bird

66

A former Midland set, unusually stabled at Worcester, 12th April 1969. Unfortunately it is not possible to read the destination plate with any degree of certainty, although the vehicles can at least be identified as M60091, M60741, and M60731. The reason for a complete train being located here is unknown with the only feasible suggestion having been a special working,

R.C.T.S.' Collection CUL 3259 / 3257 /3258

The twelve car up morning Pullman service from Bristol, accelerating past the yards at East Depot, 17th August 1967. The loadings on the 12-car morning and evening Bristol services are unknown, although some indication is given by the fact that, if one of the sets was not available, a single 8-car set was substituted. (It was certainly never an 8+6, as multiple unit connections were never provided on the original WR trains.) The 'wells-fargo', loco hauled Pullmans had also been withdrawn by this time, so it is likely that at times revision had, of necessity, to be made to a loco hauled train of ordinary coaching stock.

P J Fowler

Opposite top - *A regular although apparently rarely photographed working, was the transfer of half-sets between the Old Oak Common, Swindon, and Bristol Bath Road. Later, one set was based at Newport Ebbw Junction for the South Wales service. An unidentified four coach formation is seen here at Horfield, north of Bristol, Sunday 18th May 1969.*

P J Fowler

Opposite lower - *Somewhat more unusual is this two coach working with an original WR power car at an unreported location. Both vehicles were, of course, fitted with driven bogies although there is no indication whether this was a journey to / from repair, or simply a depot transfer, as appeared to take place on an increasingly frequent basis post 1969. The latter was no doubt due to the reduced maintenance decree, referred to earlier. The dent in the otherwise neat front end was a common feature on a number of the power cars by this time. Running in this form, speed would also have had to have restricted, due to the limited brake force available from just the two vehicles.*

David Birt / The Transport Treasury

Above - *In complete train formation, the 8-car up South Wales Pullman passes Swindon in the last full year of Pullman operation, 26th April 1972.*

J H Cooper-Smith

Above - *The South Wales Pullman awaiting departure from Paddington, 11th March 1973, just eight weeks prior to the final use of the units.*   *D E Canning*

Below - *Paddington, 22nd January 1973. The Bristol service waits in Platform 4. Despite the fact that there is rain on the roof to give the train a sheen, the whole aura is nowhere like that of past years. Notice, too, an ex LMR power car is attached to the front of the formation.*   *Michael H C Baker*

Above - *The rear power car of the 1.15 pm Paddington working leaving Bristol Temple Meads on 19th July 1968.* G R Hounsell

Below - *Reported to be a special working, the origins of which are unknown. The location is, of course, Sonning Cutting, 15th June 1968.* J H Cooper-Smith

Above - *Near journeys end from South Wales. The up service passing West Ealing, 15th May 1969.*
J H Cooper-Smith

Below - *Another South Wales service, this time near Patchway.*
George Heiron / The Transport Treasury

Above - *According to the photographer, this was probably the last time a 'Blue' Pullman unit would traverse the Berks and Hants line. Never used for regular working, the B & H was a useful diversion for Bristol trains, which would work via Westbury should there be an obstruction or delay between Reading and Chippenham. Seen here is a special charter (details of which are unknown from Newbury to London passing the military depot at Thatcham, Saturday 24th Match 1973.*

D E Canning

Below - *Pullman service, first class.*

THE FINAL ANALYSIS

We know that commencing in the early 1950s, the individual regions of British Railways were given far greater autonomy over the services they operated. So far as the LMR was concerned, any external change was limited, whilst the Western Region decided to make a return to its beloved chocolate and cream for named trains, the number increasing beyond reasonable levels! Later, and with BRB approval, the LMR would concentrate on preparing the line out of the Euston for electrification, any interim modernisation seeing heavy diesel locomotives on schedules little altered from steam days, a situation that would continue until the mid 1960s.

From Paddington, however, the ever accelerating schedules of the late 1950s, first behind re-draughted steam locomotives and later with diesel power, witnessed a diesel hauled 100 mph 'Bristolian' introduced in 1959. True, keeping the line clear for a one off service was still not easy, but it enabled Paddington to once more stamp its independence. Not for no reason was the title 'Great Western Region' being spoken of at the 'Kremlin' – 222 Marylebone Road. It was in the following year, 1960, that a slower, supplementary service, namely the Blue Pullman working, was introduced over the same route. BR must have hoped that the new trains appearance alone would have been sufficient to attract patronage and, to be fair, for a while it did. But against this it is important to remember that, with dieselisation generally and even more so with the Blue Pullman, this was technology, untried as well, as far as the UK was concerned, and it was being pushed to its limit. When something did go wrong the whole train was grounded. There is little evidence to suggest that half-set swaps took place in those early days, although, as has been seen in the photographs on page 70, towards the end it was not just a half set exchange that took place, but even a quarter set. The accelerated locomotive hauled diesel services were also not immune to problems with, on such occasions, the official reference being made to 'locomotive problems', rather than describing the diesel as the culprit – see Adrian Vaughan earlier in this work.

Also what was fine in theory did not always work in practice. Yes, the Swiss designed Schlieren bogie fitted to the new Blue Pullman performed admirably in mainland Europe But there conditions were different, compared with the UK where they were placed under a coach bristling with traction motors, auxiliary engines and the like. G Freeman Allen in his book *The Western Since 1948*, refers to the length of the vehicles also being a factor when compared with their continental cousins, but this is perhaps hard to comprehend. For one who never travelled on the trains, the present writer is forced to refer to the accounts of others, all of which appear to criticise the ride quality in one way or other. Even after the adjustments, referred to in the first chapter were made, it was still not perfect, evidence pointing to the ride quality deteriorated as service miles increased.

But if Freeman Allen's conclusions are correct and it was the extra weight dictated by the design of the British train that made the difference, surely certain vehicles would have been better than others? There is no definite evidence to support this and we are left with one inescapable conclusion, the bogies may in themselves not have been ideal. But the condition of the track was a greater factor.

We know also, from Michael Farr's comments quoted in the original book, that within a few days of entering service, paper doyleys were placed between the cup and the saucer on the new Bristol Pullman to reduce 'crockery rattle'. Less could be done to supress the venetian blinds making a similar sound in between the double glazing. But remember this was on "Brunel's billiard table" – the Western Region. What it must have been like for those on the Midland line is perhaps left to the imagination. Instead, all credit goes to those who persevered by attempting to address the ride issues and also to the paying passengers, and the stewards. There is an undoubted skill in being able to serve soup, gravy and coffee in the equivalent of a Force 8. (No doubt in consuming them as well.)

This was also a time when new designs of locomotives and stock (including the Blue Pullmans), were being built straight off the drawing board, in varying numbers and without the opportunity to evaluate a prototype in service. Yes, there were undoubted successes,

Left - *Looking almost like a toy train, a birds-eye view of Reading on 18th August 1971, with the down Swansea Pullman approaching the station, whilst a Class 47 heads the 4.15 pm Worcester to Paddington, crossing from the relief onto the up main.*

G P Cooper

but equally some manufacturers witnessed spectacular failures. The trouble was that BR had, with its modernisation programme, what was in effect an open cheque-book for a while and understandably any commercial organisation was keen to take advantage of this. I deliberately do not use the word 'exploit' in this context. Just as important was the fact that none of these manufactures had the facility to conduct exhaustive tests beforehand. It could even be argued that to have done so would have played into the hands of a rival. This, then ,was perhaps the saddest part. Some of the technology used in the new trains was untested, whilst in other areas, notably the power units, it might be considered already outdated. Regretfully neither would ever truly catch up.

In the same book, Freeman Allen, sets great store by the staffing difficulties affecting the trains, at a time, remember, when trade union power was far stronger than 40 years later. He refers to the introduction of the Midland Pullman service as having been delayed by some months until the issue was resolved. This is an interesting comment although a side benefit may have been to allow some of the modifications to the ride quality in the time available. What we do not know, is when the original service entry date for the LMR might have been, likewise we can only speculate on the ride the trains might have exercised in their true original form.

The Blue Pullman trains were in reality a victim of their own design. A style and a concept that harked back to individuality, offering a select service to a minority, rather than a 'one size fits all' which was the direction in which British Railways and society generally was slowing heading.

What is still hard to grasp is the waste of opportunity that occurred subsequent to 1967. The year before, in 1966, certainly as far as the regions were concerned, it appears that it was they who were dictating policy to BRB, rather than being compelled to tow the party line. "If it suits what we want, we shall take it….otherwise we will be put every obstruction in the way…". Consequently obstructions were put in the way of potential new services rather than the opportunities being taken. Two examples readily come to mind, the first a Plymouth Pullman, where the WR dictated that they considered a Blue Pullman set incapable of taking the south Devon banks. But this conclusion was based on an 8-car set, how about one of the redundant 6-car trains instead? The same power, 2,000 hp, but now divided

between just six vehicles. With further thought, it appears that the Southern lost an opportunity not to replace the Bournemouth Belle with a more modern variant. Certainly not long term, and perhaps not running at the same speed as the electric service, but why not in the same type of schedule as the old steam working? It might well have ensured a further decade of life for the Pullman's, perhaps to the mid rather than the early 1970s. What is hard to understand and has never been satisfactorily answered, is how BR themselves saw the future of the trains. In 1960 there was already in existence a timetable for completion of the West Coast electrification. Did they consider Blue Pullman could run in competition, to Manchester and Birmingham but by different routes, or had they simply not looked beyond the mid 1960s? The latter is hard to believe, but with thought appears ever more likely.

Charles Fryer, in his book *British Pullman Trains*, suggests a rake of modern coaches, perhaps even painted in a modern style and hauled by a few dedicated locomotives, might have been a better option. For the time he is undoubtably correct, certainly this would have allowed for greater flexibility in working and probably removed the need for the stand-by 'Wells Fargo' sets. BR's argument for multiple unit operation was that if effected a reduction in turn-around times, but this should not have been seen as the sole governing factor. Twenty years on, with changing traffic and operational patterns, perhaps the idea of locomotive hauled stock might have appeared out-dated. But remember Blue Pullman appeared in 1960, a train with a potential life of 20 years. There was no need to constrain it to a reduced life, purely due to vagaries of operating fashion.

Interestingly, the locomotive hauled Pullman cars that would replace the Blue Pullman service on a Euston – Manchester train from 1966 onwards were also built by Metropolitan-Cammel, but not with Metro-Schlieren bogies. Perhaps BR should have considered a multiple-unit electric Pullman for this route – or will someone now find information to prove they once did?

'Blue Pullman' – the prefix 'Blue' is used far more in written form that it was used in operational terms, where the trains were the 'Midland….Bristol…Birmingham Pullman', was a product of the age. Viewed today, 40 years on, the whole appearance is one from the 1960s and consequently those of us who remember that period, even though we may not have travelled on the service, recall it for what it was, stylish, modern and with the latest fashion statement – no fuss. No doubt there were those who observed the trains and wished that one day they too would be able to enjoy the luxury of such travel. They would, in HST, just a few years later. Here was indeed the 'one size fits all.'

To those who did travel Blue Pullman, it was a statement of the era, a visual indication of success or position in society. It would be interesting to consider what, in 1955/56, BR may have hoped to gain from the new trains. Financial return, credibility, kudos, perhaps even a mixture of the three. With hindsight it is hard to see how a true financial return might have been envisaged. Perhaps it was a means of advertising, a glimpse into the future, a 'concept train'. In the same way motor manufactures nowadays produce concept cars. Viewed as such, Blue Pullman was a success. Where it fell apart was when the trains had later to fit into the corporate image. When repainted, the individual style was lost, the cost of a few cans of paint being far more expensive than might have been realised. Also the fact that the builders received no further orders, not just from BR but from elsewhere, implies that prospective purchasers were not perhaps as gullible as might have been believed. (It has never been established if BR ever considered a further stand-by set, to reduce the reliance on loco-hauled stock. No doubt availability prevented the new 1960 loco hauled Pullman coaches being considered as a stand-by set as well.)

By 1973 and it was amazing that the sets were still running. Some we know, cannibalised, whilst in the end any hope for a reprieve or further use at home or abroad, was always unlikely. Had they survived, there is every likelihood that some would have found a long term use in the growing late 20th and 21st century tourist market, but in 1973 that era was too far into the future. Blue Pullman was a product of the 1960s, and was like much from that era, destined to be discarded on the alter of ever changing fashion.

In store at Swindon, the power car from a former Midland Pullman set leads an 8-car rake dumped alongside the main line. By this time the other vehicles had been concentrated in store either at Old Oak or Bristol Bath Road. This particular set remained at Swindon until, it is believed, sometime in 1974, Possibly with a hoped for reprieve, sale to a foreign operator - as was discussed in the original book, or possible purchase by a group within the UK. As is of course known, nothing came of either and sale would instead be to the scrap-merchants.

Dennis Rapley

Part of the complete train that remained stored at Swindon in 1973/74. Identification is not easy, but it is possible this was the set used for the final working,

Post 1971 views of a single 6-car set operating are rare, although it is believed the 12 car combination was still operative until at least the autumn of 1971. For the final few months three trains were available, all of eight cars. One of these was in original WR formation, another was similar, but with the substitution of an LMR power car and third was a mixed 8-car rake, part WR and part LMR stock, reported as formed thus: DMBS, MPS, TKF, TPF, TPF, TPF, MKF, DMBF. According to information on the excellent website www.railcar.co.uk, this last formation may have been used for the Bristol workings following the demise of the two individual 6-car sets.

Mileages for the trains, either individually per region, or in total have never been located.

Dennis Rapley

Page 81, top left - *June 1968, WR Power Car W60095 being shunted at the Pullman Shed at old Oak Common. The brackets for conventional oil lamps show up clearly in this view. These were only ever used for a tail lamp, in the early years of operation.*

Page 81 top right - *The rear end of Trailer Parlour First W60744, complete with signed blanking plate. Recorded at Old Oak Common in June 1968, either just prior to or after returning from service as a part-set.*   *Derek Everson*

This page, lower view - *Old Oak Common, 1969 and an interesting comparison in liveries. A repainted 8-car WR is on the left whilst to the right is a 6-car set; or at least a part pf one, still in original Nanking Blue and white. A green Brush Type 4 (Class 47) reposes to the right.*

Opposite - With freshly reversed livery, power car W60099, again inside the specially built Pullman shed at Old Oak. The designation for the South Wales Pullman appears on the blind. We still do not know why the WR power cars were fitted with a small additional window in the left hand door of the Guard's compartment, although compare also with the view on page 78 and it would appear that this modification was also made to least one ex LMR power car whilst working on the WR.

Above - From the end designation, we know this is a Trailer Parlour First, whether on its own or at the end of a 'half-set' is not known. The view was possibly recorded at the same time as that on the left page. It is known that, at some stage, towards the end of their lives, the interior of at least one car was used in the filming of a ladies lingerie advert.

Derek Everson

This page, upper - *W60094 as part of one of the three surviving complete train sets at Old Oak in May 1973.*

Derek Everson

This page, lower - *Bristol Bath Road. With a former LMR six-car set stabled, circa 1973.*

Dave Waldren

Opposite, upper - *Almost the last working to depart from Swansea. An unidentified 8-car set leaving for London. On at least one occasion in the final years, the up service was diverted to run via Westbury, using the east chord and the Berks and Hants line to Reading.*

P. Trotter

Opposite, lower - *In pseudo corporate livery at the other end of the system; departing from Paddington. In the opposite direction and certainly in the final years, the catering staff would 'shut-up shop' at Reading on both the Bristol and South Wales services.*

Opposite, top - *Withdrawn part sets at Old Oak Common.* Neil Ruffles

Opposite, lower - *Old Oak Common, circa 1969. Seen today, the front end design naturally appears dated, although in 1960 it was certainly the latest fashion statement. To be fair, any attempt at streamlining, aerodynamics, was more for visual effect than a serious attempt at reducing wind resistance.*

This page, top - *Dejected and already displaying evidence of vandalism, Old Oak Common.* Derek Everson

This page, lower - *Yesterday's prestige train, now relegated to the product as today's unwanted product. The sets were eventually dismantled by T W Ward of Briton Ferry and G Cowen at Swansea.* P Trotter

ACKNOWLEDGEMENTS

As before, many individuals have been generous in their assistance with material for this work, several having contacted me in consequence of the first book and for this I am ever grateful. In alphabetical order and with sincere apologies to anyone omitted;

Malcolm Botham, Julian Bowden, Peter Brumby, Alan Butcher, Terry Bye, Roger Carpenter, Bill Chapman, Peter Dobson, Stephen Ellingham, Derek Everson, Antony Ford, Ray Gomm, Lawrence Hassall, Ivor Lewis and the Historical Model Railway Society, Charles Long, Stuart MacKay, Wayne Marshall, Richard H F Moore, John Palk, Neil Ruffles, P Trotter, Adrian Vaughan, Dave Waldren and Mike Williams.

BIBLIOGRAPHY

The following published works have also been consulted; 'Modern Railways' April 1967, 'Railway World Annual' 1979, 'Blue Pullman' by Kevin Robertson, published by Kestrel Railway Books ISBN 0954485963.

ADDENDA TO THE ORIGINAL WORK

The term 'Blue Pullman', appears to have been rarely used in official circles, Instead 'Midland Pullman' and 'Diesel Pullman' were used. Alternatively the destination followed by the word Pullman.

Page 55 - It is suggested that painted as well as drop in letters, may have been used on the carriage sides.

Page 130 lower view, the set shown is not of LMR origin.

Page 149 - It can be confirmed the power car seen is indeed No 60091, with No 60097 behind.

Less that thirteen years of service in total and already this London bound train, near Wantage Road on 10th April 1965, is approaching five of them. Decades later it is hard to rationalise the way in which the Blue Pullman managed to go from the flagship BR service to the trains nobody wanted.
Les Elsey